pet

BEAD

David and Penny Glover

SEA-TO-SEA

Mankato Collingwood London

first published in 2008 by
Sea Publications
Lookout Drive
th Mankato
Minnesota 56003

Copyright © Sea-to-Sea Publications 2008

Printed in China

Library of Congress Cataloging in Publication Data:

Glover, David, 1953 Sept 4-.
    Bird / by David and Penny Glover.
        p.cm. -- (Owning a pet)
    Includes index.
    ISBN-13 978-1-59771-058-9
    1. Cage birds--Juvenile literature. I. Glover, Penny. II. Title. III. Series.

SF461.35G58 2006
636.6'8--dc22

                                            2005057550

9 8 7 6 5 4 3 2

Published by arrangement with the Watts Publishing Group Ltd, London

Series editor: Adrian Cole
Series design: Sarah Borny
Art director: Jonathan Hair
Picture researcher: Kathy Lockley
Special photography: Ray Moller
Illustrations by: Hannah Matthews

The author and publisher would like to thank the following people
for their contribution to the production of this book:

Les Rance of The Parrot Society, Thomas Moore, and Helen Newman.

Acknowledgments:

Stephen Bigg/Maurice's Pet Stores, Amersham, UK 12.
Bill Coster /N.H.P.A. 24 bl. Stephen Dalton/N.H.P.A. 24 br.
Mick Freakley 9 tr, 9 c, 16 bl, 19 b, 20 t, 20 c, 21 t, 22 b, 22 t, 23 b.
Colin Hawkins/Alamy Images 29. Jim Holmes 6 c.
Ernie Janes/N.H.P.A. 10 br, 10 tl.
Roy Miles Fine Paintings/ Bridgeman Art Library London 7.
Ray Moller title page, 5, 11 t, 11 b, 13, 14, 15, 16 tl, 17,
18, 18 t, 19 t, 21 b, 24 t, 26, 27 c, 27 b
Kevin Schafer/ N.H.P.A. 4 r. Harald Theissen/Alamy Images 28.
(c) 2004 Topham Picturepoint 6 br.
Terry A .Tuxford 4 tl, 8 bl, 16 br, 20 b, 23 t, 27 t and Cover.
Zoological Society of London 25.

Contents

Pet birds

**Some birds make excellent pets—
they are colorful, lively, and intelligent.
Keeping a pet bird is extremely rewarding,
but it is an important responsibility, too.**

Wild birds live everywhere—
emperor penguins survive in the
freezing wilderness of the
Antarctic, while bee-eaters live
in the hot forests of Asia. Bird
species vary in size and shape,
from tiny hummingbirds to
huge ostriches, the biggest birds
of all. An ostrich is too large to
make a suitable pet, but there
are many bird species that do.

*Hummingbirds are beautiful to watch in
the wild, but should not be kept as pets.*

DUTY OF CARE

RSPCA International has outlined five basic
rights which should be granted to all pets:

- **Freedom from hunger and thirst**

- **Freedom from discomfort**

- **Freedom from pain, injury, and disease**

- **Freedom to express normal behavior**

- **Freedom from fear and distress**

What a bird needs

Pet birds are not wild—they rely on
their owners to provide them with
somewhere safe to live. They need
fresh water, the correct food,
attention, and exercise. Their home
must be kept clean, and if they get
sick, they must be taken to a vet.
Birds are sensitive living things and all
owners have a duty to care for them.

Why do I want a pet bird?

This is a good question to ask yourself. Not everyone likes birds. Birds can bite or squawk loudly, so they are not as cuddly, for example, as a cat or dog. Some people are even scared of birds when they fly. However, if you enjoy looking at birds, and are prepared to give up some of your free time every day, then a bird may be the pet for you.

RSPCA

RSPCA International works with animal welfare organizations in more than 60 countries worldwide. The association scheme has helped governments and organizations update their animal welfare laws. This has safeguarded the future of thousands of animals at risk.

A budgie gets to know its owner. Most budgies will perch on fingers, respond to whistles and noises, and may even learn to talk!

Birds and people

For thousands of years people have valued domestic birds for their eggs and meat, while decorative birds were kept for their attractive songs and colorful plumage.

DOMESTIC BIRDS

About ten thousand years ago, the first farmers settled in villages to grow crops and rear animals. Along with goats, pigs, and cows they bred birds on their farms. As well as meat and eggs, domestic birds provided feathers for making pillows, arrow flights, and quill pens. Hens, ducks (left), geese, and turkeys are common domestic birds today.

WORKING BIRDS

For centuries people have harnessed the remarkable abilities of some birds. Before the invention of the telephone people used homing pigeons to deliver messages. They were also used by soldiers during the Second World War (1939–45). The soldiers wrote messages on tiny slips of paper and attached them to a pigeon's leg. When the carrier pigeon was released, it flew home, traveling hundreds of miles in just a few hours.

DECORATIVE BIRDS

Colorful feathers and beautiful songs have always made birds popular pets. Victorian landowners imported peacocks from India to decorate their country gardens. Linnets, nightingales, and canaries were popular for their singing powers. As recently as the 1970s, songbirds were taken from the wild and kept in tiny cages. This is a cruel practice. In many countries it is now illegal to take birds from the wild, or to import endangered species from abroad.

Sweet Sounds, 1918 by John William Godward (1861–1922).
In the past, pet birds were treated like toys or tools, rather than live animals. They were often kept in a poor environment, such as the tiny cage shown in this picture.

CITES

In 1975 the Convention on Trade in Endangered Species of Wild Fauna and Flora (CITES) came into force. It has helped reduce the trade in endangered birds, including many species of parrot, parakeet, and cockatoo found in the Amazon region. However, many birds are still dying as a result of habitat loss.

Choosing a bird

There are more than 9,000 species of wild bird in the world. Selected bird varieties have been carefully bred from just a few of these species to produce birds that can be kept by people as pets.

Budgies

Budgies, or budgerigars, are small members of the parrot family. Since they were first bred, more than 150 years ago, their lively behavior and intelligence has ensured they remain the world's number-one pet bird. Millions of budgies are kept as pets worldwide!

All wild budgies are green with yellow markings. By careful selection, through many generations, budgerigar breeders have produced a whole range of "fancy" varieties, including the "pom-pom" budgie shown on the left.

BUDGIE

A good choice as a first pet bird?	**Yes!**
Difficulty level	**Easy**
Entertainment value	**High**
Lifespan	**7 years**
Sociable birds?	**Yes!**
Intelligence level	**High**

BUDGIE OR KEET?

Don't get confused between a budgie and a parakeet. Although many people argue that they are the same, the word parakeet is often also used to describe several types of small parrot. Just remember that a budgie is a parakeet, but not all parakeets are budgies!

CONSERVATION ALERT!

You should never take birds from the wild, or buy a bird taken from the wild. Exotic species, such as the scarlet macaw, are endangered by illegal collectors. Trapped wild birds are treated cruelly and most die even before they are sold. Birds kept as pets should have been bred in captivity by a reputable breeder.

Canaries

Canaries originate from the Canary Islands and are a popular choice for a pet bird. Most people choose to keep canaries for their beautiful song. Canaries are not as intelligent as budgies and will not learn to recognize and respond to you in the same way. They also don't like to be handled as much. Like budgies, canary breeders have produced a whole range of canary varieties by selective breeding.

CANARY

A good choice as
a first pet bird?.......................... **Yes!**
Difficulty level .... **Easy**
Entertainment value................ **Medium**
Lifespan .... **10 years**
Sociable birds?..........................**Yes!**
Intelligence level.................... **Medium**

ZEBRA FINCH

A good choice as
a first pet bird? .... **No!**
Difficulty level .... **Medium**
Entertainment value................ **Medium**
Lifespan.................................... **5 years**
Sociable birds?......................**Yes, very!**
Intelligence level............................ **Low**

Zebra finches

Zebra finches are tiny colored birds that like to live in groups. They can be kept outdoors in a small aviary with other sociable small birds, though they will need extra heat and light in cold weather. They cannot be tamed and handled like larger pet birds.

Other species

LOVEBIRD

Lovebirds are available in lots of different colors.

A good choice as a first pet bird?	**Yes!**
Difficulty level	**Medium**
Entertainment value	**Medium**
Lifespan	**25 years**
Sociable birds?	**Yes, very!**
Intelligence level	**Medium**

Lovebirds

Lovebirds are colorful small parrots that make excellent pets. They are very sociable and should always be kept in pairs. They can be kept indoors, but they are larger birds than budgies and canaries, and need as large a cage as possible.

COCKATIEL

A good choice as a first pet bird?	**Yes!**
Difficulty level	**Medium**
Entertainment value	**High**
Lifespan	**20 years**
Sociable birds?	**Yes!**
Intelligence level	**High**

Cockatiels

Cockatiels originally come from Australia. They are very friendly and soon learn to talk. Cockatiels like to be stroked and may preen your eyebrows in return! These lively birds need a cage at least 20 x 20 x 24 in (50 x 50 x 60 cm). Ideally cockatiels should be kept in pairs. You can keep just one but you must spend lots of time with it.

Cockatiels are intelligent and can be taught to say words.

LARGE PARROT

A good choice as
a first pet bird? .... **No!**
Difficulty level .... **High**
Entertainment value .... **High**
Lifespan .... **30+ years**
Intelligence level .... **High**

Larger parrots and cockatoos

Large birds, such as macaws and cockatoos, are wonderful creatures full of character and intelligence. But they are very demanding pets and need a great deal of attention. If they don't get it, they may become very destructive and difficult to handle. For this reason parrots and cockatoos are not a good purchase as your first pet bird.

Small parrots, such as this Australian King parrot, can be a real handful, but make great companions. They are not really suitable for a first pet.

When you visit a breeder's aviary take a list of questions with you. This will help you to remember what to ask.

Buying a bird

Whatever species you choose to keep, start by getting advice from an expert. People at your local bird club will recommend the best birds for you and put you in touch with reputable breeders. They can also show you how to handle and care for your bird. Go to see a breeder with an adult. Make sure the aviaries are clean, the adult birds (parents) are healthy, and the young birds come with a breeder's written guarantee.

A safe home

Your bird's cage is the main part of its environment. It sleeps, eats, and spends most of its time there, so it is vital that your cage matches the needs of your bird.

What size?

Birds are active animals, and they need to stretch their wings. Always choose as large a cage as possible, with at least two perches (not placed one above the other). The bar spacing is also important. If it's wrong your bird could damage its wings or become trapped.

Finches	17x30x18 inches (45x76x45 cm)
Canaries	17x24x18 inches (45x60x45 cm)
Budgies	17x17x24 inches (45x45x60 cm)
Cockatiels	20x20x24 inches (50x50x60 cm)
Lovebirds	24x24x24 inches (60x60x60 cm)
Parrots	24x35x48 inches (60x90x120 cm)

Minimum cage size (wxlxh) according to bird

CAGE DO'S AND DON'TS

DO place the birdcage in a room where your bird has company, but not so that it can be easily scared by loud noises, etc.

DO make sure cats and other pets cannot get to the cage.

DO make sure the room can be made safe for your bird to leave the cage for exercise.

DON'T stand the cage in a cold draft, by an open fire, or in bright sunlight that will overheat your bird.

DON'T put the cage in the kitchen. Cooking smells, fumes from nonstick cooking pans, and sudden changes in temperature may harm your bird.

"There should be enough room for your bird to fly from one perch to the other, turn easily, and fly back again."

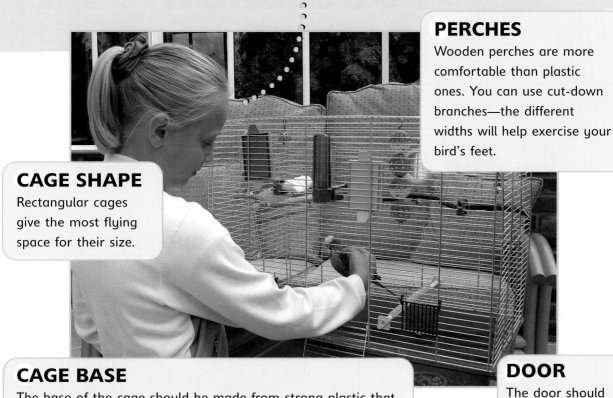

PERCHES

Wooden perches are more comfortable than plastic ones. You can use cut-down branches—the different widths will help exercise your bird's feet.

CAGE SHAPE

Rectangular cages give the most flying space for their size.

CAGE BASE

The base of the cage should be made from strong plastic that is easy to wipe clean—don't choose one with a wire bottom. A sliding tray makes it easier to remove droppings and spilled food from the bottom of the tray. This should be done every day. To absorb moisture the tray should be lined with bird-sand or paper, not sawdust or cat litter (both can cause a bird to have digestive problems if eaten).

DOOR

The door should be easy to open and close, but shut securely.

TOYS

Birds, especially budgies, are curious and enjoy investigating toys, such as bells and mirrors. They also like to exercise on ladders and swings. But don't overcrowd the cage. It is better to change toys around occasionally than to provide too many at once.

OUTDOOR AVIARY

As your interest in bird-keeping grows, you may want to establish an outdoor aviary. Aviaries have a "flight" in which the birds have plenty of space to fly and feed, and a shelter where they can roost comfortably at night. You can also provide your birds with plants for shade, or even to nest in.

Food and water

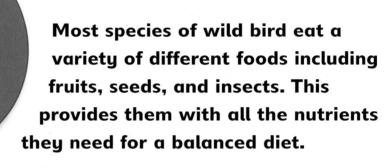

Most species of wild bird eat a variety of different foods including fruits, seeds, and insects. This provides them with all the nutrients they need for a balanced diet.

The diet of a pet bird is based on seeds (shown right), fruits, vegetables, and meat, such as water-packed tuna. Ask your vet or at your local bird club. They will be able to help create a diet specifically for your bird. One thing all experts agree about is that you should never feed your bird "treats," such as chocolate or potato chips. Chocolate is poisonous to birds and chips contain high levels of salt.

Many birds also enjoy eating cooked corn on the cob, hard-boiled eggs, fresh zucchini, and cheese.

Canaries don't like citrus fruit. Check with your vet about what fruit to give them.

"Complete" balanced food for your bird is available from pet stores. Always check first with your vet about the suitability of these. Many do not provide the correct nutritional balance.

"Put food in strong, plastic containers that your bird won't be able to knock over easily."

MEAL TIMES

Most experts recommend that you feed your bird twice a day—in the morning and evening for about half an hour—instead of leaving food out. Make sure you change your bird's food at the same time every day, and make sure it eats. Never leave food in the cage to get moldy; this could spread disease.

OBESITY PROBLEMS

Monitoring your bird's weight is essential. Obesity can cause serious health problems, including breathing difficulties. Small birds, such as finches, need 1/4 to 1/3 oz (6–8 g) of seed per day. Budgies need 1/3–1/2 oz (8–12 g). And don't forget fruit and vegetables.

WATER

Your bird must always have fresh water to drink. Without water it will die very quickly. Clean and refill your bird's water container every day. Watch to make sure it is positioned where your bird can perch to drink from it easily.

New skills

Getting to know your new pet bird is an exciting time. It is important to spend time with your bird so it recognizes you and becomes tame as it grows older.

Bonding with your bird

Don't pester your new bird too much. If you feed and talk to it at the same time each day, it will gradually get to know the routine. Move slowly and quietly as you change the food and water in the cage, so you don't scare it. Offer the bird tidbits to eat, holding them still until the bird is confident enough to take them.

Catching and holding

Sometimes you will need to catch your bird, perhaps to trim its claws. Put your hand in its cage and wait until your bird has settled on the cage floor. Hold your hand open over the bird and, when it's still, grasp the bird gently but confidently.

Hold your finger next to your bird on its perch and talk gently to it. Your bird will gradually get used to you. Eventually it will perch happily on your finger as you talk to it.

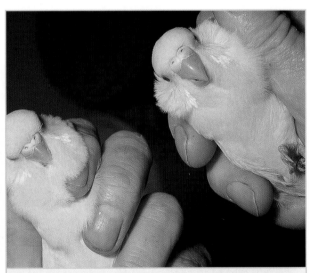

Hold the bird so that its head is between your first and second finger. Larger parrots have a powerful bite and should be handled with gloves or by an adult.

"Yo-yo was attacked by his mother and lost a lot of flight feathers. He'll be able to fly again next year when they grow back."

Flight time

To keep your bird healthy, it is essential to give it exercise by letting it out of the cage to fly around the room. First you must make the room safe. Make sure the doors and windows are closed, there are no other pets in the room, and the fireplace is blocked with a guard.

Open the cage door. Let your bird come out on its own—it may be nervous at first. Leave the cage door open so your bird can return to the cage when it is ready. It will go home when it wants to eat or drink.

"You've got to have patience when teaching a bird to talk."

LEARNING TO TALK

Budgies and parrots are wonderful mimics. Follow these steps to start your bird talking:

- Be patient. Teaching a bird to talk is not as easy as it sounds. Try a young bird for the best results
- Practice talking to your bird regularly
- Start with simple words, such as hello
- Repeat the same sounds or words as you talk to your bird
- If your bird says a word, say it back to reward it
- Some people train their bird to say their address, in case it ever gets lost

Staying healthy

Fresh food, clean drinking water, a clean home, and regular exercise will help keep your bird healthy. Some beauty treatment is needed too—your pet bird will look forward to a bath and manicure!

Good hygiene

Germs need warmth, moisture, and a source of food to multiply. A damp mixture of old food and droppings in a birdcage is the ideal place. Regular cleaning will keep germs at bay. Don't forget to clean the toys and perches. Make sure you are clean too! Wash your hands before and after handling your bird—humans are the number-one germ carrier.

Droppings and food will stick to the perches and cage bars. At least once a week, or as soon as you see the cage getting dirty, let your bird out for some exercise while you give the cage a good scrub with nontoxic detergent. Make sure the cage is thoroughly dry before you let your bird back in.

Keep the bottom of the cage fresh and dry. Clear up spilled food and water daily. Change the bird paper or sand as soon as it becomes soiled.

BIRD MANICURE

Like your nails, a bird's claws never stop growing. If they become too long they make it difficult for the bird to walk or perch. You can trim the claws yourself if you have clippers and a clotting agent. But if you are not confident, ask a vet to do the job.

Never use sandpaper on perches to wear down your bird's claws. It doesn't work and will only make its feet sore and possibly cause an infection.

Beauty bath

Birds need to keep their plumage clean and neat. If they have broken or ragged feathers they cannot fly. To encourage your bird to preen its feathers provide it with a large, heavy dish of lukewarm water. Some birds like to bathe more often than others. Start off by giving your bird a bath once or twice a week. Adjust the number of baths according to how keen your bird seems.

Many birds also enjoy being sprayed. Use a new plant mister on your bird to simulate rain. It will flutter its wings to catch the water.

Through the year

At certain times of the year, your bird will need special care. Like birds in the wild, pet birds respond to the seasons. In the breeding season your bird will be more lively. This is when it will look its best.

SPRING

Spring is the season when birds mate and rear their young. As the mating season approaches, a cock bird will display its beautiful plumage and sing loudly. Hens start nest-building. A young budgie hen may lay eggs on the floor of the cage, though if she has not mated with a male they will not hatch.

Keep two hens or cocks together so you don't have any unwanted eggs. Irresponsible breeding is cruel.

SUMMER AND FALL
Molting

Molting and growing new feathers uses a lot of energy. Not only will your bird be quiet and subdued, it will look scruffy and feel sorry for itself!

Most birds molt once a year. They lose their feathers and a new set grows. This ensures that any damaged feathers are replaced, keeping the bird's plumage in good condition for flying. Molting usually starts toward the end of summer and may last for up to six weeks.

"Don't forget to plan your pet care in advance of your vacation. Don't leave it to the last minute."

This indoor flight has been fitted with additional heaters and lights.

During molting it is a good idea to provide extra vitamins and minerals. Most pet stores sell food with special supplements for feeding your bird during the molt.

Summer is the time when most people go away on vacation. If you are planning to go away, make sure you arrange for someone to look after your bird. Leave the carer a list of instructions. Don't forget to leave the vet's telephone number in case of an emergency.

WINTER

In winter some species, such as finches, need extra heat and light. Make sure your bird is not exposed to the cold or too near a radiator where it could overheat. Some birds like their cage covered, which helps keep out drafts. Most aviary birds will need to be brought in from the outdoors.

Leave your bird with someone you trust, like a relative or neighbor. Before you leave, make sure they understand all of your instructions.

Breeding birds?

As your interest in birds grows, you may want to breed and show your birds. However, you should only breed birds if you know the babies will have a home.

Breeding birds should only be attempted when you feel confident you can look after more birds. Obviously, you need a cock (male) and at least one hen (female) to breed from. But you also need somewhere to breed them, perhaps a shed that can be converted or a bird-proof garage. The hen should be at least 12 months old, and the cock 10 months.

Keep breeding pairs and chicks under close observation. Budgies don't mind being disturbed in their box.

Breeding season

Springtime is the breeding season, when your birds will become increasingly active. Before putting a cock and hen together, provide them with a suitable nest box or pan and nesting material.

NEST BOX

The size of the nest box will vary depending on the birds. Budgies need a minimum of 8x5x6 in (20x12x15 cm), with a hole of about 2 in (5 cm). Face the hole into the corner of the cage to provide the birds with some privacy. Put a layer of wood shavings in the bottom.

The egg numbers and incubation times of birds vary. Canaries, for example, usually lay a clutch of four or five eggs, which hatch after 14 days. The adults feed the chicks for four or five weeks, until they can feed themselves.

Young budgie chicks fledge (emerge from the nest box) when they are about four weeks old. Their parents will feed them for several more weeks.

Show birds

If you want to show your birds it is a good idea to join a local club that specializes in your chosen species. There are strict rules for showing exhibition birds, so you should take advice from experts. Many people do not believe that birds should be shown. This is because they feel it causes the birds too much distress. However, if undertaken correctly, showing your birds can be a good way for you and your birds to socialize—birds love all the attention of the judges.

Budgies lay four to six eggs, which hatch after about 18 days. While the adults are feeding their chicks, you should provide rearing food. This should include seeds soaked in water to make them soft, and fresh greenstuff.

Budgie on parade. You can learn a great deal from other exhibitors at bird shows. Their wealth of bird-keeping experience can often help solve any problems of your own.

Watching birds

Even if you do not have the time or space to keep a pet bird of your own, you can still get pleasure from watching and helping other birds.

Attract birds to your backyard by putting out wild bird food. A bird table helps keep the birds safe from cats while they feed. Both small and large birds will peck at seeds and fat on the table. Feeders attract small perching birds such as chickadees and finches.

This starling is having a refreshing bath to help keep its feathers clean.

Bird feeders like these are especially important during the winter when other food is scarce.

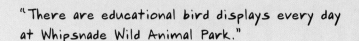
Exotic birds

You can see many beautiful and exotic birds, such as these scarlet macaws, at places like Whipsnade Wild Animal Park in the UK, or the San Diego Wild Animal Park in California. At Whipsnade, special bird shows give you an opportunity to see these magnificent birds in full flight, swooping and climbing over the spectators. These carefully arranged shows are also a great way to learn about the behavior of these spectacular birds, and why their conservation is so important. The bird keepers answer hundreds of questions every week!

SCARLET MACAW

Scarlet macaws are a protected species because their numbers in the wild are decreasing. However, people still illegally capture macaws for the pet trade, which is why it is important to buy your pet bird from a reputable breeder. The best place to see a macaw is at an animal park or zoo.

25

A sick bird

If your bird's behavior changes suddenly it may be very sick. It is a bird's natural instinct to hide any illness. In the wild this would help it avoid being attacked by predators.

SIGNS YOUR BIRD IS ILL:

- Green droppings
- Swelling around the eyes
- Loss of energy
- Dull feathers
- Sitting on the bottom of the cage
- Weight loss
- Lack of appetite
- Retching
- Growths around the beak or feet
- Swollen feet or joints
- Discharge from the nostrils or sneezing

Many bird experts believe that one day of sickness for a bird is the same as seven days for a human. So, if you are concerned about your bird, take it to your vet immediately. The vet will examine your bird and ask you about its symptoms. How has the bird's behavior changed? Has the bird eaten anything unusual?

Examine your bird regularly to help spot any problems early on.

"Young birds are particularly vulnerable to infections. Their behavior must be closely monitored."

Sadly, this young budgie is very sick. The problem has been caught in time, so it should make a good recovery.

Diagnosis

When the vet has diagnosed the problem he or she will tell you how your bird should be treated. The vet may recommend a change in diet, or give you some medicine to add to your bird's water. You can help reduce problems by keeping everything very clean. You should also keep your bird's vaccinations up to date.

WORMS

Worms are difficult to detect and there are many types. Worms usually cause weight loss, weakness, or breathing problems. If you are in any doubt, take your bird (in its cage) to your vet. He or she will be able to use the droppings to make a diagnosis and treat your bird (right).

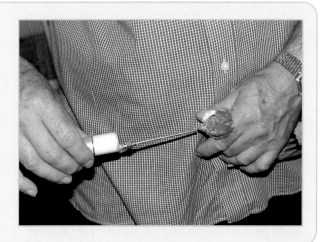

MITES

If your bird is preening far more than usual, it may be infected with feather mites. Take your bird to the vet who will treat it with a spray (left). Preventative treatments for mites are available for use at home. Check with your vet to find out which is best for your bird.

Losing a pet

If your bird escapes or if it dies, the experience can be very traumatic. As long as you have taken good care of your bird you shouldn't blame yourself.

IF YOUR BIRD ESCAPES

You should do everything you possibly can to prevent your bird from escaping from its cage. This can simply be making sure the cage door is securely fastened at all times. If your bird does escape outside you must act quickly.

- **Put the cage outside with the door open**

- **Make sure there is plenty of your bird's favorite food on offer**

- **Try calling its name—a budgie will usually respond within a few minutes if it hasn't flown too far**

- **If all else fails notify your local pet rescue center—someone may come across your bird and bring it in to the center**

Terminal illness

Your vet will only suggest putting your bird to sleep if nothing can be done to cure it. There is nothing easy about saying goodbye to your pet bird for the last time. But if your bird is terminally ill, it will suffer more while it is alive.

Some people bury their pets at special pet cemeteries.

Get someone to take photographs of you and your bird, or take some yourself.

Taking time to remember

The death of a pet is very upsetting. You will feel a whole range of emotions, from anger to guilt. Take time to look at photographs of your bird and think about the good times you shared together. You could draw a picture or even write a story or a poem about your bird, or about how you are feeling.

Old age

It is a fact of life that, eventually, your bird will die of old age. But this doesn't make it any easier to cope with, so it's important to ensure you provide the best possible care during the time that you have together.

AFTER THE DEATH OF A PET

DON'T rush out to buy a new bird. Also, don't accept a new bird from a friend or relative. Take time to consider all your options.

DON'T make the mistake of trying to replace your bird—that will never happen. Apart from anything else, a new bird will have a different personality.

DO think about your surviving birds. If you had a pair, then the surviving partner will also be missing your bird.

DO check how the rest of your family feels. You might be over the grieving process, but maybe they aren't, especially if you have any younger relatives.

Glossary

Diagnose: To find out what is wrong.

Disease: A serious illness, bad health.

Distress: Pain, disturbance, or discomfort caused by bad care.

Endangered species: A species whose numbers are becoming so low it is threatened with extinction.

Environment: The surroundings in which a bird (or any other creature) lives.

Exotic: Unusual—from a very different part of the world.

Generations: The successive stages of a family of living things. Parents are one generation, their offspring are the next.

Illegal: Against the law.

Infection: A disease that is passed from one living thing to another, often by germs.

Mimic: To copy or imitate.

Minerals: Salts and other substances that, in small quantities, are an important part of the diet.

Molt: To shed and regrow feathers, fur, or skin.

Mite: A tiny spiderlike animal that lives in birds' feathers and on other animals.

Nontoxic: Not poisonous.

Nutrients: The different components of food that give an animal energy and help keep it well.

Obesity: Being overweight.

Plumage: A bird's feathers.

Predator: An animal that hunts other animals.

RSPCA: Royal Society for the Prevention of Cruelty to Animals.

Terminally ill: Having an illness that will cause death.

Traumatic: Shocking or very upsetting.

Vaccination: An injection to protect against some diseases.

Vitamins: Substances that are present in small quantities in foods that birds and other animals need to stay healthy.

Websites

Throughout the world there are many specialist bird clubs whose members breed, show, and share information about their chosen bird species. Your local pet center can provide information about local groups. Information is also available on the Internet. Some useful websites are listed below:

www.budgerigarsociety.com/
This is the website of The Budgerigar Society, the largest specialist society for bird breeders in the world. The society issues rings for show birds and supports more than 300 bird shows each year. It also runs a Pet Owners Club for those who keep budgies as pets.

The Real Macaw Parrot Club
www.realmacaw.com
The Parrot Society of New Zealand
www.parrot.co.nz
These websites feature lots of information on a wide range of parrots, care guides, news, and FAQs.

Zebra Finches on the Internet
www.zebrafinch.info
This website features news articles, a buying guide and FAQs.

The African Lovebird Society
www.africanlovebirdsociety.com
This website is full of advice for keeping and caring for all nine types of African lovebird.

The National Cockatiel Society
www.cockatiel.org
The Scottish Cockatiel Association
www.scottishcockatielassociation.co.uk
The websites of these societies feature breed guides, and tips for keeping and training cockatiels.

More general information on the care, health, and welfare of pets is available from a number of organizations. These include:

www.rspca.co.uk
The RSPCA website has links to RSPCA websites throughout the world. It is full of information about animal adoption, news, care, training, and education.

www.hsus.org
The Humane Society of the United States' website offers pet-care guidance to help you maintain a long and rewarding relationship wth your pet. It offers information on issues affecting pets, pet adoption advice, animal shelters, and related news and events.

www.petsinamerica.org
This website tells the story of our lives with animals at home. It also lists events and programs relating to the Pets in America exhibition as it travels across the U.S.

www.aspca.org
This website of the American Society for the Prevention of Cruelty to Animals. This organization lobbies for humane laws to protect animals and offers pet owners information and advice.

Every effort has been made by the Publishers to ensure that these websites contain no inappropriate or offensive material. However, because of the nature of the Internet, it is impossible to guarantee that the contents of these sites will not be altered. We strongly advise that Internet access is supervised by a responsible adult.

Index